THE INCA

A TRUE BOOK®

by
Stefanie Takacs

Children's Press®
A Division of Scholastic Inc.

New York Toronto London Auckland Sydney
Mexico City New Delhi Hong Kong
Danbury, Connecticut

An ancient
Inca road

Reading Consultant
Jeanne Clidas, Ph.D.
*National Reading Consultant
and Professor of Reading,
SUNY Brockport*

*The photograph on the cover
shows the ruins of Machu
Picchu. The photograph on the
title page shows Quechua
children at the ruins of
Sacsahuaman.*

Library of Congress Cataloging-in-Publication Data

Takacs, Stefanie.
     The Inca / by Stefanie Takacs.— 1st American ed.
          p. cm. — (A true book)
     Includes bibliographical references and index.
     Contents: Before the Inca — Inca rule — Life in the Empire — Great
buildings, artisans, and scientists — Skilled farmers — End of the Inca.
     ISBN 0-516-22776-9 (lib. bdg.)   0-516-27823-1 (pbk.)
     1. Incas—Juvenile literature. [1. Incas. 2. Indians of South America.]
I. Title. II. Series.
F3429.T215 2003
985'.019—dc21
                                                          2003004536

1 2 3 4 5 6 7 8 9 10 R 12 11 10 09 08 07 06 05 04 03

Contents

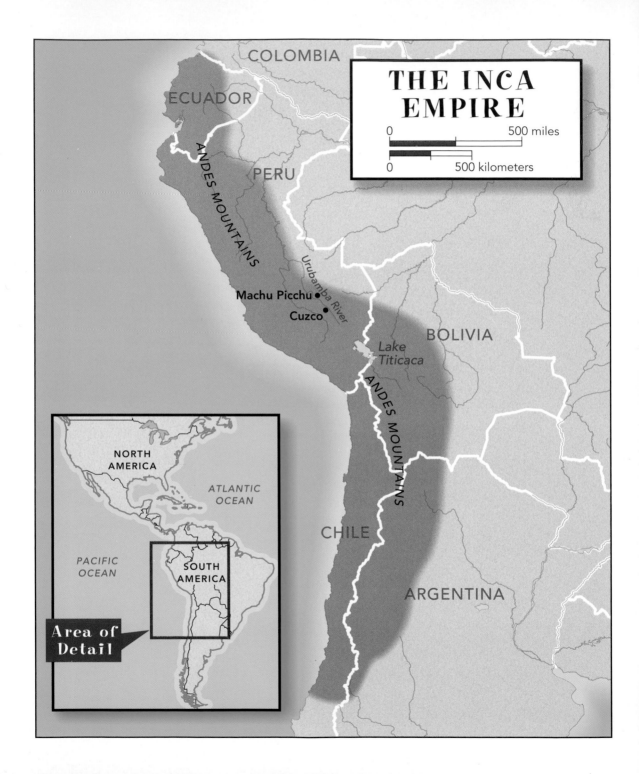

Beginnings

The Inca (IN-ka) were a group of people who came to the Cuzco (KOOS-ko) Valley, high in the Andes Mountains of South America, about one thousand years ago. Over the next few hundred years, they built a large kingdom. At its peak, the kingdom stretched along the

The high, cold plains where the Inca settled are called the altiplano.

Andes Mountains from what is today Ecuador to Chile.

Many other peoples lived in the region before the Inca, including the Moche (Mo-CHAY), the Paracas (Pa-RA-cas), and the Tiwanaku (Tee-wa-NA-koo). These peoples were long gone by the time the Inca arrived. The Chimu (CHEE-moo) and the Qolla peoples lived at the same time as the Inca and were eventually **conquered** by them.

There are a few legends that tell how the Inca people came to be. One says that around A.D. 1200, a man named Manco Capac and his three brothers and four sisters emerged from a cave near Cuzco. They decided to seek **fertile** lands that would make them rich. Eventually, they reached a green valley high between two mountains. Manco Capac threw a golden rod into the valley to see if it was fertile. It sunk several feet into the ground, and the Inca knew they had found their home.

Manco Capac claimed the land and called the new city Cuzco. He named himself the Inca, or king. He called his people *capac-cuna* (ca-PAC-coo-na),

According to Inca legend, Manco Capac was the first Inca (above). He is said to have founded Cuzco, which became the capital of the Inca Empire (right).

or "great ones." Today, we refer to all people who were part of this kingdom as Inca.

The Inca Empire

For about two hundred years, the Inca lived as farmers and herders. Gradually, they spread out to occupy all of the Cuzco Valley. In the 1400s, the Inca began conquering other peoples in the land surrounding the Cuzco Valley. Their ninth ruler, Pachakuti,

took power around 1438. He started a great **empire** by conquering more and more people.

During the rule of Pachakuti (right), the Inca Empire spread south to the Lake Titicaca region (below).

The Inca Empire soon spread south to Lake Titicaca and north to the Urubamba

River. Throughout the next century, the empire continued to grow. At its largest, it included more than twelve million Andean people.

The Inca called their kingdom Tawantin-suyu, (Ta-WA-tin SOO-yoo), which meant Land of the Four Parts. Each of the four parts of the empire had its own governor. The governor was always a relative of the Inca king and took his orders from the king.

These are the ruins of an Inca fortress built in the 1400s in what is now Ecuador.

In the central part of the empire, the Inca rulers used an unusual system to maintain control over their people. They organized people according to the numbers five and ten. Each governor ruled over two or three district governors, and each district governor ruled ten thousand households. Two village leaders,

The ruins of an ancient Inca home in the Andean highlands

each responsible for five thousand households, reported to each district governor. This system of rule continued downward, with households divided into groups of one thousand, five hundred, one hundred, fifty, and ten. In this way, the king controlled all the people in his empire.

In Inca villages, people lived in groups of related families. These groups were called *ayllu* (AY-yoo). The people lived in houses made

Today, Andean women carry their babies on their backs just as Inca mothers did hundreds of years ago.

of stone and **adobe** and shared land, animals, and food.

The Inca also had a **unique** way of keeping records. They had no written language.

The Language of the Inca

These people still speak Quechua, the language of their Inca ancestors.

The official language of the Inca people was Quechua (KEH-choo-ah). No one knows what the Inca spoke before they spoke Quechua. As the Inca had no written language, there are no clues to help solve that mystery. Quechua is still spoken by the Andean peoples of Peru and Bolivia. Here are some words in Quechua:

English	Quechua	English	Quechua
baby	wawa (wa-wa)	house	wasi (wa-see)
bridge	chaka (cha-ka)	man	ghari (gar-ee)
corn	sara (sa-ra)	woman	warmi (war-mee)
dog	alg'o (al-ko)		

Great Builders

The Inca were skilled road and bridge builders, **artisans,** and scientists. In total, the Inca constructed more than 25,000 miles (40,000 kilometers) of roads. The Inca traveled these roads on foot. They did not have horses and did not know about the wheel until Spanish

The Inca built thousands of miles of stone roads high in the Andes Mountains.

explorers introduced it to the region in the 1500s.

One of the main uses of the Inca roads was to pass along information. The Inca did this with a messenger system. Runners called *chasquis* (CHAS-kees) were stationed for periods of time in shelters along the roads. These shelters were 1.5 miles (2.4 km) apart. Each chasqui ran information to the next shelter and passed it to the chasqui who lived there. This was done until the news reached its **destination**. Amazingly, with this system, news could travel 1,250 miles (about 2,000 km) in five days.

The Inca made suspension bridges similar to this one to help them cross mountain rivers. This modern rope bridge is connected to original Inca stonework.

Sometimes, the Inca had to build bridges over the mountain rivers. The Inca's greatest bridge was 148 feet (45 meters) in length, **suspended** high above the Apurímac River. They called this bridge *huacachaca*, (wa-ka-CHA-ka), "the holy bridge."

Inca workers also built impressive buildings and cities. Sacsahuaman (Sak-sa-WAH-man), a ceremonial center and fortress

The ruins of Sacsahuaman, a ceremonial center and fortress near Cuzco

outside Cuzco, was started in the 1400s. It took thirty thousand workers more than seventy years to complete the fort. Another magnificent building in Cuzco was Coricancha (Koo-ree-CON-cha). It was a golden temple decorated with fountains, corn plants, and life-size llamas, all made of gold.

Inca artisans were highly skilled. They crafted beautiful items made of silver, gold, and gemstones. Other artisans made fine cloth and ceramics.

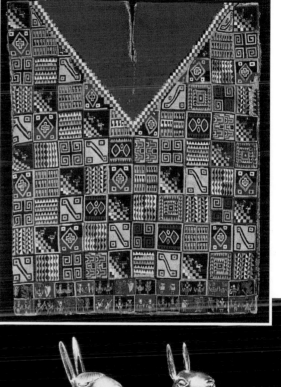

The Inca crafted beautiful items of gold (top left), finely woven cloth (top right), wood (above), and silver (right).

This stone gate shows Inti, the sun god and the most important of the gods worshipped by the Inca.

Inca priests studied the sky and the seasons. They used their understanding of the sun, moon, and stars to help them create a calendar.

This carved rock at Machu Picchu served as a kind of calendar. The shadow cast by the tall column of rock showed the change in the sun's path over the year.

The calendar was important for farming and religious purposes. The Inca also studied medicine and knew how to fix broken bones.

Skilled Farmers

Some of the success of the Inca Empire was due to the farming techniques of the Inca. They knew how to make **canals** to bring water to dry places. The farmers also cut flat **terraces** into the steep hillsides and planted crops on them. This allowed the water

Many of the
Incas' terraced
fields are still
in use today.

to seep into the ground where
the crops were planted rather
than run down the slopes.

Maize, a type of corn, was
the most important crop. Inca
farmers also planted potatoes,
squash, tomatoes, peppers,

cotton, peanuts, beans, and grains. The potato was the most important **staple** food because it grew even in the cold mountains. The Inca used the chilly mountain air to dry the potatoes out after they were harvested. Once the potatoes were completely dry, the Inca made flour from them.

In addition to growing crops, the Inca raised animals. Guinea pigs, alpacas, llamas, dogs, and ducks are some of the animals they kept. From llama and

Potatoes, one the Incas' most important foods, are still a staple crop for people of the Andes Mountains (left). Like the ancient Inca, the Andean people today use llamas to carry loads (right).

alpaca hair, the Inca got wool. They used this and cotton to make cloth. The Inca also used llamas for carrying heavy things and for meat. Llama dung was used to fertilize the crops.

The End of the Inca Empire

The end of the Inca Empire came soon after Spanish explorers arrived in South America. The Spanish had heard stories of the Inca gold and set out to find it. These *conquistadors* (conquerors) reached the west coast of South America in the late 1520s.

Spanish explorer Francisco Pizarro leading his men through the Andes on their way to meeting the Inca

Meanwhile, the Inca Empire started to fall apart. After the Inca king Huayna (WHY-na) Capac died in 1528, two of his

A statue of Atahualpa, the last Inca king

sons fought for control. Finally, the son named Atahualpa (A-ta-WAL-pa) won in 1532. He would be the last Inca king.

In November of 1532, a Spanish explorer named

Francisco Pizarro asked the new king to meet him for a friendly visit. Pizarro tricked Atahualpa, however. When the two leaders met, Pizarro's soldiers attacked the Inca.

Pizarro and his men capturing Atahualpa

The Spanish defeated the Inca and captured Atahualpa. Atahualpa stayed alive for nine months by promising to give the Spanish gold and silver. After getting the treasure, however, the Spanish killed Atahualpa anyway.

In November of 1533, the Spanish marched into Cuzco. With their powerful weapons, they ended the hundred-year-old Inca Empire.

The Spanish also brought European diseases to the

The Spanish marched into Cuzco
and crushed the Inca Empire.

region. The Inca had never
been exposed to these diseases
and their bodies had no way to
recover from them. Thousands
of people died, and the Inca
Empire was destroyed.

The influence of the Inca culture can still be seen in the weaving methods and fabrics of the Andean people today.

However, many reminders of the Inca Empire remain. Today, Inca ruins exist in the Andes Mountains of Peru, Bolivia, Ecuador, Chile, and Argentina. Inca arts, crafts, and designs can still be seen in the weaving, ceramics, and jewelry of the peoples who now live in these regions.

In addition, many people living in the mountains of Peru and Bolivia still speak Quechua and use ancient Inca

Farmers in the Andes Mountains weed with the same kind of short, wooden hoes that their Inca ancestors used.

farming practices. They also grow the foods and crops their **ancestors** grew. Although the Inca Empire ended almost five hundred years ago, its **legacy** continues today.

The Ancient City of Machu Picchu

Hiram Bingham during an expedition to Peru in 1912

There were some Inca cities the Spanish explorers did not find. One of them was Machu Picchu (MA-choo PEEK-choo). It was a royal country estate high atop a mountain near Cuzco. It remained hidden until Hiram Bingham, a professor from Yale University, rediscovered it in 1911. By then, it was in ruins.

Important Words

adobe brick of sun-dried earth or clay

ancestors relatives who lived in the past

artisans artists or craftspeople

canals human-made waterways

conquered defeated by use of force

destination place toward which someone is traveling

empire large territory or group of territories under a single ruler or government

fertile able to produce good crops

legacy something valuable left behind

staple basic food

suspended hung from a support

terraces raised, level spaces with one or more sloping sides

unique one of a kind

Index

Meet the Author

Stefanie Takacs has worked in social services, youth education and programming, and educational publishing. She has written numerous educational books on reading-test preparation and Native American peoples. Stefanie holds a bachelor's degree in liberal arts and a master's degree in educational psychology.

Experiencing new cultures is part of Stefanie's life. She has lived in Africa, South America, and the United States. She has also traveled extensively through the United Kingdom and Europe. These days Stefanie can be found in the Bronx, New York, or in the Litchfield Hills of Connecticut, where she enjoys gardening, reading, writing, running, painting and drawing, and being with her family.